BLUEBERRY CLOUDS

BLUEBERRY CLOUDS

RITA BOUVIER

THISTLEDOWN PRESS

© 1999, Rita Bouvier
All rights reserved

No part of this publication may be reproduced or transmitted in any form or by any means, graphic, electronic or mechanical, including photocopying, recording, or any information storage and retrieval system, without permission in writing from the publisher.

Canadian Cataloguing in Publication Data

Bouvier, Rita E.
Blueberry clouds
(New leaf editions. Series six)
Poems.
ISBN 1-895449-97-9
1. Indians of North America—Canada, Western—Poetry.
I. Title II. Series
PS8553.0883B48 1999   C811'.54   C99-920195-6
PR9199.3.B625B48 1999

Cover illustration by J. Forrie
Typeset by Thistledown Press Ltd.
Printed and bound in Canada

Thistledown Press Ltd.
633 Main Street
Saskatoon, Saskatchewan
S7H 0J8

 Canadian Heritage / Patrimoine canadien

Thistledown Press gratefully acknowledges the financial assistance of the Canada Council for the Arts, the Saskatchewan Arts Board, and the Government of Canada through the Book Publishing Industry Development Program for its publishing program.

This book is dedicated to Matthew Joseph Jacoby,
ocapana¹   *Flora And Joseph Bouvier,*
omoshompana²   *Louis Opikokew,*
ohkompana³   *Albertine Bouvier*
and all the rainbow children of the world.

---

¹his late great-grandparents
²his late grandfather
³his late great-aunt

CONTENTS

Nimoshom and I	9
Blueberry Clouds	10
Leaving Home	11
Kistapinanik	12
An Outstretched Hand	13
When Hope Is Lost	14
Blasphemy As Resistance	17
Two Hundred Dollar Advice And More	18
Kayas Mana	19
A Sacred Life	20
Kimamanow Iskwew	21
Reflections of Flora	22
Music In My Mother's Movement	23
Iles le Bouleau to Mazatlan	24
Running Dream	25
The Medicine Man	26
A Good Story To Tell	27
The Double Double Wedding	29
I Dreamed You	31
In a Sea of Babies I Found You	32
Taming A Monster Moose	33
A Pickle Day	34
I Am A Frog	36
A Conversation With Peter Gzowski	37

Kikinaw	39
Land Is The Politic	41
Mamaskach Oma	42
Sounds Without Meaning	43
Nimanitou	44
When Time and Space Collapse	45
Kamamawapinow	46
Lost To The Casino Blues	47
Wollongong Sky	48
A Science Dialogue In India	49
Just Another Barroom Conversation	51
Epikwetamapiyan	52
Remembering Will Have To Do	53
On The Old Northwest Trail	54
Sometimes I Find Myself Weeping At The Oddest Moment	55
Lac La Ronge Night	56
The Dancing Fish Knew	57
On The Reserve	58
One More Sad, Sad Note	59
Light Breaks	60
Poetry	62
A Crisis in Identity	63
I Write	64

Nimoshom° and I *Cree for "my grandfather"*

"Caw, caw, caw
the crows are calling
N i t a n i s° *Cree for "my daughter"*
it is time
to begin the day
we will be home
when the sun
is straight over our heads
and I will fry fresh *dore*° *French for walleyed pike.*
over the open fire *The language spoken by the*
Nitanis *Métis had many nouns in French.*
the tastiest part will be for you"

The sun is just peeking
over Big Island
mist rising off the lake
Nimoshom and I set out
"There is a perfect spot
over there," he points
a slight movement
of his lips and chin

We stop to set our net
I point the canoe
towards the mainland
the church steeple my guide
It is the same journey we take
after the nets are cleaned
dried and mended
it is reassuring to know
what is asked of me

It is reassuring to hear
my grandfather's voice
"*Ekosi ekwa, Nitanis* *Cree for "This is it for now*
kawetak ekwa"° *my daughter, let us go home now."*

Rita Bouvier

Blueberry Clouds

With a clamour we climbed
out of the boat
our freshly washed red
shamrock lard pails in hand
hoping to get the best
spot for a blueberry
picking day. Plink-plink
sounds everywhere.
The first to fill theirs
would feast on fish cheeks
on a spread of willow branches
when the work was done.

Beside the open campfire
we shared blueberry stories
and *Moshom*° always knew   *Cree for "grandfather"*
the proportion picked-eaten
blueberry clouds on our faces.

Peyikwaskwan°   *Cree meaning "the clouds*
the clouds are beginning to swell   *are beginning to swell"*
he'd say
it's time to head home
when he made us laugh
we knew it was time.

Leaving Home

Nimoshom° is standing   Cree for "my grandfather"
cap in hand
waving good-bye
a yellow bus
with me in it
leaving Sakitawak°   Cree name for Ile a la Crosse
lake on Missinipi°   Cree name for Churchill River
the big water   meaning big river
Kistapinanik,°   Cree for Prince Albert, Saskatchewan
my destination   meaning "the place of high office"

reassurance
is a story
he was there
a long time ago
working for Revillion Frére°   French fur trading company
after the family broke ties
with the Hudson's Bay Company

and then he expressed
hope for the future
that a way of being
would not be lost
that place
would not be forgotten
that a language
would not be lost
Nitanis, ahpotikwimina   Cree, meaning "perhaps you will
kamistahitimisoyon°   think you are better than others"

such sadness
in his voice
I never forgot

Rita Bouvier

KISTAPINANIK° *Cree name for Prince Albert,*
Saskatchewan meaning
friendly suburban faces *place of high office.*
remind me
of my first primer
All Around The Neighbourhood
streets lined with trees
houses in a row

I am hypnotised
by a promise
but first I learn
my cousin Linda
is not my sister
my grandmothers
are not
except *Kokum*° *Cree for "grandmother"*
my mother's mother

I learn to hate
this brown
I learn to hate
the seeming weakness
of people, like *Moshom*° *Cree for "grandfather"*
I hate so much
I hate myself
C a n n i b a l i s t i c
I am *Wetiko*° *Wetiko, a powerful being*
the hungry one *who lives by himself/herself*
 and eats its victims

I nearly destroy everything
Moshom taught me

An Outstretched Hand

an outstretched hand
greets me home
a gesture
that nourishes
like sunshine to a wild rose

you stand
at the edge
of the schoolyard
an outstretched hand
afterwards
there will be
taunting you really are not
my father
as I have named you
since I can remember

When Hope Is Lost

I am perplexed
by a home visit
a school
has asked me to make
I arrive reluctantly
the scene of a party
now over
children fast asleep
a woman
who reminds me
of my mother
offers me
the only chair
and I have forgotten
why I came
we drink tea
and I tell her
who I am
her children's teacher
"*Moshom,*
namoyanikiskeyitin
tansi tasicikiyan"°   "*grandfather, I am no*
     longer sure what I
Moshom listens   *can do to help*"
and then speaks

"*Kayas oma Nitanis*°   Cree for "*a long time ago,*
we were returning home   *my daughter*"
from a long season
collecting furs
we had just passed
Portage La Loche
the sun was setting
as we rounded the bend
on the river
a perfect spot

for a rest
we were out of rations
after we set camp
we left
in search of food
Nestow awa° Isidore   *Cree for "my brother in law, that is"*
headed North
Ekwa niwichiwagun,° Samuel   *Cree for "and my friend"*
went South
Nistis awa,° Eugene   *Cree for "my brother, that is"*
He went East
Ekwa niya Nitanis°   *"And myself, my daughter"*
I headed West
we returned
empty-handed
ready to settle
for the night
silently,
we made a fire
to warm our bodies
we drank *le thé muskeg°*   *Mechif for "Labrador tea"*
to settle the rumble
in our stomachs
the sky was darkened now
we strained our eyes to see
when all of a sudden
we spotted four partridge
at the light's edge
cast by campfire light
Ah Wah! Wah! Nitanis°   *An expression in Cree to express joy*
it was a joyous occasion   *in this context*
feasting and storytelling
we went to sleep that night

Rita Bouvier

where the partridge came from
no one knows for sure, *Nitanis*"

"*Astam ota*"°, he motions   *Cree for "come over here"*
come and sit closer beside me

BLASPHEMY AS RESISTANCE

on our early morning tour
of the graveyard
Moshom° is telling tales   *Cree for "grandfather"*
of saints and sinners
each marker a tale
that only he can read
ringing with laughter
while *Kokum*° scolds   *Cree for "grandmother"*
his blasphemy
stories of people
now dead
less then perfect lives
stories of priests
dirty secrets
less than holy lives

something is comforting
redeeming
about this place
my cousins and I follow
to hear every detail
and *Kokum*'s scolding

Two Hundred Dollar Advice And More

dress to be included
dress for the position
you aspire to . . .
dress for comfort
dress for authority
put dollars waist up

dress with quality
the colours of class
blue, grey,
black, camel
red for power
green, maybe
avoid dress
with busy lines

complete your look
a pair of simple shoes
eeeeelskin, perhaps
finishing touches
of real stones
in your jewellery
hair and makeup
accessories
matching hair
pay
to look the part

on my way out
the morning paper read
The food bank needs your help

Kayas Mana°

Nitanis kayas mana°
wealth was a measure
of all our relations°
moshom° is telling me
as he slips a dollar
into my hand

° Cree for "a long time ago"

° Cree for "a long time ago now, my daughter."

° The concept of "all my relations" refers to all living things. "All living things" in Cree is extended to all of nature.

° Cree for "my grandfather"

A Sacred Life

she slips bare the suit of armour
that protects her daily movements
each item removed carefully
and placed deliberately
on the rack to avoid creases

she walks barefooted
to feel the energy of a wood floor
alive as the forest that provided
she draws water from the tap
cupping a life-giving force
smoothing over every inch

she dries her body sacred
in the presence of hope, a little boy
in the presence of love, a man
she picks flowers to cover herself
ready to step to another time

KIMAMANOW ISKWEW° 　　　　　　　Cree/Mechif for "Our mother is the
　　　　　　　　　　　　　　　　　keeper of the fire"

She gives life
her gentle way guides
provides quietly
steps aside on the first step
but we know she is there

nismis° *was found*　　　　　　　　Cree for "my younger sibling"
with only a nightshirt
running a winter storm
running a winter storm
bruised and beaten blue

beaten and left to die
she is leaving home
to reclaim herself
buried in a happy time
she cannot remember

REFLECTIONS OF FLORA

beside the warmth
of a pot-bellied stove
Kokum° weaves tapestries   *Cree for "grandmother"*
earth
grass
sky
blood
she raised fourteen
of her own
plus seven
I am the youngest

beside the steady hum
of a Macintosh
I spin tapestries
the colour of
love

Music In My Mother's Movement

I can tell *moshom*° is pleased   Cree for "grandfather"
with the questions I'm asking
"It's time to come home.
It will be a great summer
after a stay at St. Paul's"

"*nitanis*°," he says   Cree for "my daughter"
"wipe those tears
from your eyes
a chat with St. Peter
has assured me
a place for you
beside me,"
he jokes, I laugh
death is natural

moshom passes on
to the next world
blessed with family
his only regret
not saying good-bye
to Flora,
nimama°   Mechif for "my mother"

the news comes
she misses him
crying secretly
at night
we know
she will join him soon
and I cry
we all cry
for ourselves
returning her body
to the earth
Kiyanow oma   Cree for "it is us, now, who
kakitimakisiyak°   are impoverished"

Rita Bouvier

ILES LE BOULEAU° TO MAZATLAN *French for "Birch Island"*

I travelled here today
three thousand miles
from my birthplace
an island on the lake

in the drenching sun
a tranquil moment
under the shade of a palm tree
I imagined *Moshom*° sitting there *Cree for "grandfather"*
under the shade of a pine tree
in old age
journeying
through time and space

perhaps there are no answers
one generation to the next
in Iles le Bouleau or Mazatlan
a good path taken
is all that counts

Running Dream

I am deer leaping
over thick brush
air scented
cranberries over-ripened
earth's perfume
I have travelled here once
yet, I have never been
an arched stone way
leading from the forest
to the open sea
all around me now
the forest has fallen
a man on the road
cautions me
return, return, return
I gaze back
the forest now
a sketch of ancient ruins
a sea so green
a sky so blue

Rita Bouvier

The Medicine Man

We kept our distance
from the medicine man
stories of power
in his gaze
as we followed him
down the path
He carried a cane
in one hand
a medicine bag
in the other

To test him
I agreed to feign
a twisted ankle
His piercing
deep blue eyes
ran through me
as our eyes locked

He invited me
to look inside
offered me a potion
for my ailment
and a twinkle in his eye
whispered to me
"There is no cure
for your condition"

A Good Story To Tell

the plane flies low
above the treeline
the watchful ones
like brother beaver
warn in siren voices
"the police are coming
the police are coming"

women and men
run in all directions
some to tall bushes
some to makeshift sheds
some to the houses
hiding their *chipwegees°*   *Cree for "homebrew"*

Albertine, the only one
not caught
by the excitement
her washing machine
loud and motorized
has drowned out
the warning cries

out of gasoline
she wonders
where the children are
whereupon she spots
two tall uniformed men
coming her way

quickly to the closet
she runs, heart pounding
grabbing the *chipwegees*
"where *nimanitou°*?" she cries   *Cree for "my God"*
God hardly caring
into the washing machine
she dumps it all
and not too soon

Rita Bouvier

there is a knock at the door
the police are wondering
where the children are
the smell of homebrew
filling their nostrils
their faces gleaming
flash a search warrant

Albertine can't read
they search knowingly
and not a drop is found
in the form of evidence
as they walk away
Albertine pours tea
she can hardly wait
to add her story

THE DOUBLE DOUBLE WEDDING

Smoke circles
as he lights his pipe
I can tell It will be
one of those stories
"*Kayas oma Nitanis*°　　　　　　　　*Cree for "It was a long time*
Nihiyawak°　　　　　　　　　　　　*ago, my daughter"*
had their own ways　　　　　　　　*Cree meaning "the exact*
the missionaries it seems　　　　　　*speaking people"*
did not believe this was so
I have heard this story told
of a great chief
a great hunter loved
the missionaries thinking
they could win souls
invited *Kistapo*°　　　　　　　　　*"Sits in High Office"*
and his friend, *Napesis*°　　　　　　*"Little Boy"*
to their tent one evening

This is how it was told to me
now I am telling you
so you can tell others

the story is told
the missionaries offered
Kistapo and his friend, *Napesis*
this new religion
promises of heaven
the happy hunting ground

Tapwe oma Nitanis° *Moshom*° offers　　*"This is true, my daughter"*
　　　　　　　　　　　　　　　　　　　Cree for "my grandfather"
It is true, of course
Kistapo and *Napesis*
understood such promises
cannot be made in this world
but *Kistapo*, no fool
took their offer

29　　Rita Bouvier

to 'marry' him
and his companion
of many winters
in the Springtime
when they returned

so it is told, Nitanis

during the Winter
as Spring drew near
Kistapo and *Napesis*
would be seen
meeting secretly

in the Spring
the priests returned
as they said and
prepared for a ceremony
a double wedding
as requested by *Kistapo*
and his friend, *Napesis*
a feast would follow
as custom in that village
the priests noticed
a festive air in preparations
cupped hands hiding laughter
and amusement like children

the wedding ceremony done
the priest's curiosity aroused
God's ways worked wonders
asked *Kistapo* and his wife
to join them that evening
and so it was
they came to understand
that *Kistapo* and *Napesis*
had traded wives.

That is the story as it was told to me, Nitanis

I Dreamed You

I dreamed you
yesterday time
You were dreaming
a little boy
his mother
there tomorrow
Did you feel me
holding you closely
my body cupped in yours?

IN A SEA OF BABIES I FOUND YOU

I edged my way
to the nursery
in a sea of babies
I found you
crying helplessly
I lifted you
pressed you close
to my warm breast
warm blood
streaming your face
from a scratch
on your left cheek
"*Nigosis°*," I cried   *Cree for "my son"*
warm tears
streaming my face

Taming A Monster Moose

A monster moose
lives under Matthew's bed
he claims
it only comes out
at nighttime
slowly we tame the moose
we discover
in a story
it is a bull moose
who is afraid of daylight
and little boys
"There is nothing to fear,"
Matthew reassures
"we can share
potato chips and coke
I'll take care of you
you are not to worry."
last night,
a monster moose
kissed Matthew
as he fell asleep.

A Pickle Day

"I want you to come to school today Mama
It's immunization day,
I want you to be there
just like you were
when I was little"
my big boy of seven begs me
Immunization is a big word, I think

"I can't but
I'll be there in a story," I offer
"I have dreamed a story for you.
It is titled,
The Pickle Who Had a Bumpy°

There once was a pickle
who had an owy
because he had a bummmmmm pee,
get it?
He was feeling very sorry for himself
And so went for a walk,
bump-bump, bump-bump
Along the way
he met a carrot
Carrot, he said
I'm sad because I have a bumpy
Carrot said
you think you have problems
My skin is peeled,
I've been sliced and diced
He was not going to get sympathy
from Carrot
And so he walked further
until he met Broccoli
Broccoli, he said
I'm sad because I have a bumpy
Broccoli said

° *This story was written in cooperation with my son Matthew.*

you think you have worries
My legs have been chopped
and all that left of me
Is my head,
don't tell me your troubles
And so he walked further
until he met Potato
Potato, he said
I'm sad because I have a bumpy
Potato said
you think you have problems
I've been cooked through and through
And so he walked further
and he met . . .
now you finish the story" I said.
"And he met Pork chop.
Pork chop, he said
I have an owy-bumpy
And Pork chop chased him
and ate him up."

I Am A Frog

a cold January day
returning home
I call out to anyone
who will listen
"Did anyone miss me?"

and you cry out
"Mama, she's home"
delight in your voice
helps me turn the corner
preparation of food
now an act of love

you appear suddenly
at the top of the stairs
announce
you are a frog
you need a kiss
from Princess Mom
to turn you into
the Prince you really are

I reach out
slow motion
to kiss you
on the forehead
and I whisper
"I love you
little creature-inside"
as you run away
and the moment
disappears
too quickly

A Conversation With Peter Gzowski

I was born
into the world
speaking Mechif
a language
whose base is Cree
with a whole bunch
of French thrown in
for good measure
Kipaha la porte!° I say   *Mechif for "Close the door."*
I grew up on an island
livelihood based
on the land
hunting, fishing
and trapping
I wanted to be a teacher
like Sister Biseault
when it happened
I am not sure
this feeling of separation
the coming apart
and I am a chameleon
blending for safety
changing
to escape hostility
a hierarchy
based on the colour
of one's skin
as teacher
I could not teach
the facts
of the history text
simultaneously
there was rejection
from my own
It didn't make sense
until we spoke

37   *Rita Bouvier*

our voices poisoned
understanding
doesn't make
day to day living easy
the disease
that destroyed
the spiritual core
of humanity
robbed me and you
of a place to live
it continues
under a new name
globalization
havoc on the whole
for a rich few
now
a beautiful little boy
frames my view
of the world
and I tell him
he has great responsibility
because
he has the gift
of the rainbow
that will split the beam
of thinking, of being
that separates
me from the other
me from place
me from time
me from a man
who is father to my son

I am sorry, Peter
I've spoken too long

KIKINAW°   Cree for *"Our home"*

Kikinaw is
a sacred place
we meet
at the end of day's toil
we come together
hearts meeting minds
our disembodied selves
converging
and now we are one
we tell a hero's story
because we are
we enter
without baggage
we leave it outside
"You can always pick it up
on the way out,"
a voice echoes

Kikinaw is
a place of resistance
we don't have to be
the ones
who walk in shame
of the colour we wear
here, we are
the most beautiful
here, our mothers
and fathers
hold places of honour
here, the children
are creation's gift
here, the music
of our communion
fills the spaces

Rita Bouvier

here, we imagine
never leaving
this place again
But, *Kikinaw* is
a violent place
for many
worse than we know
on a street
going nowhere
that place
where we exist
only in the shadows

Land Is The Politic

land is power
land is transcendental
we cannot just talk
of land
we must *reclaim* it
land is a spiritual base
land is an economic base
we cannot just talk
of land
we must *live* on it
through our actions
we guarantee
an *indigenous* education

the destruction of land
is the politic
we must address
to reclaim our knowing
to reclaim our cultures
education does not
have to be written
we must live it
it is community life
that nurtures
not government structures

Land is the politic
we must address
internationally
Aski oma
peyakwon kimamanow°   Mechif/Cree for "the
                          earth, it is like our
                          mother"

Rita Bouvier

Mamaskach Oma°

mamaskach oma
we speak of liberation
as feminist
as Marxist
as Indigenous
and all the while . . .
our discourse hums
on a staff of competition
the notes ring with laughter
at our foolishness

° *Cree for "Unbelievable, this is" meaning what I have just heard is hard to accept as truth.*

Sounds Without Meaning

i n s t i t u *sin*
c o n s t i t u *sin*
I like the way
foreign sounds
roll off my tongue
rhyming prostitu *sin*
onomatopoeia
I like the way
it echoes in my ear
a tom-tom kind of sound
existentialism
a philosophy
I like the smartness
of this sound
enlightenment
four beats away
from beginning to end
self-determina *sin*
it does have a ring

NIMANITOU°   *Cree for "my God", used as*
             an expression of disbelief

I am to some
a walking encyclopaedia
of Native organizations
programs and people

I am to some
the archives of ancient past
fifty thousands years ago
maybe more

I am to some
the expert of the woes
of a contemporary people
dispossessed

I am to some
your local library
of obscure facts
and information
then and now
and the future
nimanitou!

When Time and Space Collapse

I think words
are extensions
of ourselves
not inherently moral
deed a language
of the body
that tells the truth

as light shifts
I am saved
by the darkness
I think only of
what is possible
and not what is
an abyss of hatred
tonight I stand
in the shadows
dark alleys of time
where I can see clearly
the lies
tonight I am tired
Rosa Parks tired
of giving in
to polite conversation
tonight I reach
beyond the stars
of the great beyond
tonight I am
part of the great mystery

KAMAMAWAPINOW *Cree for "we will gather together"*

we will sit down soon
to talk
to make plans
to ensure that
what we want
will happen
to talk theory and practice,
it is all the same
how we are related
as people
how we are related
to the land
how we are related
to the winged creatures
the two legged
and the four legged
kamamawapinow
those who are wise
will preside
over our talk
we will work the truth
bringing our hearts
and minds together
the land will be
our teacher
our guide

Lost To The Casino Blues

in the dead of winter, I'm lost
lost to the Casino Blues
in the dead of winter, I'm lost
lost to the Casino Blues
my cultural values
have gone and left me
only momentarily I console
my aching heart
when the cash, cash
comes rushing in
I'll remember who I am

"I am indigenous
I am intelligent,
I am beautiful,

so you'd better watch out"°   *Youth chant at the World Indigenous*
                                Conference on Education,
my money will be spent   *Wollongong, Australia*
for the common good
I'm above the rest
beyond the temptation
of my own addictions
I am lost, I am lost
to the Casino Blues,
to the Casino Blues

Wollongong Sky

I feel the sky closing in
when you think you know me
before we have spoken
when you dislike in me
what you don't see in yourself
when you mistake my solitude
as conceit
when you mistake my silence
as dislike for you

The truth is that
at this very moment
I can feel the power
of a vast sky
I yearn to be with someone
I can't be with today
I yearn to understand
myself — yourself
I yearn to fly with the wind
as friend in a Wollongong sky
I yearn to return to that place
so dark, so warm, so safe
I yearn to sit beside my grandfather
to hear him say, "Nitanis°"   *Cree for "my daughter"*

A Science Dialogue In India

I think
time is relative
to the experience
of the knower
I think
time is place

We arrived late
last night
in the dark
so happy
to find our names
among smiling
foreign faces
unable to find
the rhythm
of certain order
without dividing lines
from here to there
here, a place
incomprehensible
there, a place
of complete trust
somewhere
a discomforting
thought of stepping
in a different time
overwhelmed
sights sounds smells
of no return

I know
there is order

in bicycles
three-wheeled cabbies
oxen-drawn buggies

junky old cars
buses bursting people
transport trucks
pedestrians
and sacred cows
sharing the same space
without incident
the blowing horns
and waving hands
have meaning
I reassure myself
uncertain
only the affection
in your eyes
fade the lines
space and time
that separates
me from that place
I call home

Just Another Barroom Conversation

We break into Cree,
and I start laughing
the heavy sadness
of city living
now a memory
After our seventh scotch,
yours on the rocks
we try to outdo
the Inuit record number
of concepts for snow
you bet me
we have more concepts
for the types of drunks
we, Mechif/Cree can have
and I believe you
because you are my sister
we have a fun type drunk
we have a cry type drunk
we have a lonely type drunk
we have a sexy type drunk
we have an angry type drunk
we have a tight type drunk
I have stopped counting now
and yet you continue,
we have a religious type drunk
like the robed priests back home
my gut is aching so hard
with laughter
at my own attempts to mimic
the drunk types we've seen
or heard about
all the while
you act as the artistic Director
correcting body posture
movements out of place
"I'll have another
double scotch on the rocks"

Rita Bouvier

Epikwetamapiyan°

A blue moon rises
epikwetamapiyan
from the depths of longing
there is no place
that feels like home
anymore
the city has just become
another place
out of time
and the bush
is desperate
for yesterday

Cree for "I am sitting here lost — broken hearted." Its meaning perhaps is closer to describing a sense of deep longing.

REMEMBERING WILL HAVE TO DO°
(in memory of my dad, Louis Opikokew)

kayas mana°
we looked after ourselves
gardens, canning, storing
in the muskeg for winter
we helped with the chores
everyone had a job to do
we played for learning
we cooked for doing
moosehide tanning
a community activity
there was respect
for one another
children were not hit
we listened to old people
we did not talk back
you listened to children
so they would listen to you
we spoke to each other
naming as we were related
the children were always with us
learning along the way
ceremonies and games
taught us a way to be
love was the foundation
passing on our language
teaching the good life

remembering will have to do

A found poem in the voices of old people collected by the Meadow Lake Tribal Council to support the development of their early childhood program.

Cree for "a long time ago"

Rita Bouvier

On The Old Northwest Trail

The Old Ones°
sky dance
on the old Northwest trail
from Frenchmen's Butte
to *Notinto Sepik*°
a pretty jig
swishing colourful skirts
to a fiddle tune so sweet
while a distant drum pounds
And tonight, they ask
I join the circle
and we dance
and we dance
and we dance
until the dawn of city lights

A reference in Cree for the "northern lights"

The Cree place name for North Battleford

Sometimes I Find Myself Weeping At The Oddest Moment

sometimes I find myself
weeping
at the oddest moment

an unexpected voice
mon oncle Andre° "*my uncle, Andre*"
calling Christmas Day
wishing me
a Merry Christmas

and I am
that little girl
walking across the lake
with her grandfather
to check on the snares
and traps he has set
in this frost
exploding moon
in surrounding islands

the frost is biting
and he motions I walk
in the shade
of his warm body

soon he claims
we will be
in the thick of brush
and we will make a fire
to warm our bodies
drink *le thé muskeg*° *Mechif for "Labrador tea"*

Lac La Ronge Night

night is falling
deep sky blue
against a paler shade
of blue snow
swish swish swish
of ski
crisply etched
a wine-dipped pen
writing a chorus of time
as memory

on destination
we gather around
an island bonfire
roasting hot dogs
over a snap crackling
eyes on fire
wolf on edge
recording movements
occasional silence
makes us one
in spirit
howling at the moon
this time
in Lac La Ronge

THE DANCING FISH KNEW

Kayas manaº   *Cree for "a long time ago"*
long ago, this is
a life began
to write its story
a never ending story
of cycles
and movements
so graceful
it made the fish dance
to hear the story
this is true
I am telling you
as it is
as story within story
unfolded
each intersecting
it was difficult
to understand
where the story ended
where the story started
the beginning
or the end
the dancing fish knew

Rita Bouvier

On The Reserve

the sun shines
upon my face
while the songbird
thrills half the world awake
the wind rustles
singing leaves
as the soft clink
of kitchen noises
and the rhythm
of coffee brewing
tells me
Dad is awake
and *mama*°   *French for "mother"*
is nearby
on the reserve

One More Sad, Sad Note

the desecrated bodies
of dark-skinned women
are d i s c o v e r e d
in shallow graves
among a grove
of w e e p i n g willows
the papers write
of seemingly
desperate lives
without hope

the bodies
r e c o n s t r u c t e d
confirm what we all knew
the news flashing images
in black and white
awiyak osimisa°   *Cree for "someone's sister"*
a little boy's mom
kokum°'s grandchild   *Cree for "grandmother"*
one more
sad, sad entry
as historical note

Light Breaks

light breaks blue dawn
on snow-covered fields
CBC is calling
for warmer weather
welcomed news
on this wintry day

on the garden show
the folk tale
of peonies and ants
is shattered
the relationship
between the rusty nail
and coniferous tree
is questioned
thank goodness
that wisdom holds
wild berries are sweeter
than domestic berries

light breaks orange haze
tales of Oprah telling
beef stories on the air
there is news
of the Pope's visit
Havanna waiting
repressed longing

at the junction of St. Louis
and Prince Albert
the news is
that Reform is concerned
about recent decisions taken
on Aboriginal issues
which fail all Canadians
an apology for residential schools
is welcomed

but not so
for land claims
after all, the past is past
common sense
to folk like you and me
doing the thinking for us
we should be thankful
light breaks white
blessed by snow
the news breaking a story
of a man falsely accused
and someone should pay
for the wrong done
harm not retractable

for some, I think

Poetry

poetry is the fate
of the silver fox
now stretched inside-out
conforming to the shape
of it's wooden frame
the inside layer
of skin exposed
transparent
traces of wounds
tissue hardened
a healing
of some sort
a lifeline rich
yet ordinary

A Crisis in Identity

I am a Métis woman
my mother now
she is a status Indian
number 351
my sister she is
a Bill C-31
Indian, that is
my brother he is
a non-status Indian
my father is white
my dad is Indian

I am
a Métis woman,
a modern woman
in the process of . . .

I Write

I write experience
a Métis woman
a contemporary woman
in the process of becoming
I write a mirror
a glimpse of myself
if you catch yourself in me
or a part of the dance
it is intentional
I write a Shakespearean soliloquy
a lament for the human condition
I write a Smartian
By Grand Central Station I Sat Down And Wept
I write the last word
a balance
to regain locus of control
I write inspiration
a meaning, a purpose to go on
I write simply
a story that recreates